Apollo. So what possible relevance can such relics have in a world of computers and TV soap operas?

Not much, you might think, especially as some of them may have been early attempts to explain natural phenomena, something science does more accurately these days. However, there is more to most myths than simple narratives about how the world was made, or why the elephant has a trunk, or the bad behaviour of supernatural beings. Most myths are about what it means to be human.

As they tackle universal themes – courage in the face of adversity, dealing with the problems of life, learning about yourself and others – they can be endlessly retold in new ways, for every new generation. Of course, above all, they are great *stories* in the fullest sense, with terrific characters and gripping plots. They are ancient wisdom, and as fresh as tomorrow morning – enjoy!

Using this Teaching Notes booklet

This booklet provides suggestions for using the Myths and Legends to develop comprehension with children individually or in groups. Suggestions are provided for a range of follow-on activities and cross-curricular links.

In order to support planning and record keeping, the curriculum coverage chart on pages 5–7 provides curriculum information relating to the curricula for England, Wales, Northern Ireland and Scotland. This includes PNS Literacy Framework objectives, Assessment Focuses for reading, writing, speaking and listening showing what levels children can reasonably be expected to be achieving when reading these TreeTops books.

Comprehension strategies

Book Title	Comprehension strategy taught through these Teaching Notes					
	Predicting	Questioning	Clarifying	Summarising	Imagining	Deducing
Fables from Africa	✓	✓	✓	✓	✓	✓
When a Cat Ruled the World	✓	✓	✓	✓	✓	✓
Hercules the Hero	✓	✓	✓	✓		✓
King Midas and other tales	✓	✓	✓		✓	✓
How the World Began	✓	✓	✓		✓	✓
Rama's Journey	✓	✓	✓	✓	✓	✓

Contents

Introduction

The TreeTops *Myths and Legends* books contain a wide range of the oldest and most enduring stories in the world, retold by leading contemporary children's authors to bring out all of the action, drama, humour and depth of the original stories in a way that makes them as exciting and meaningful today as ever. The 24 books contain 70 traditional stories from around the world, illustrated with stunning, vibrant images in a range of styles. A thought-provoking letter from the author at the beginning of each book explains something about the background of the stories and the process of writing or retelling them. The letter also encourages the reader to make links between stories in a collection – prompting a fascinating investigation into the similarities and differences between stories that have evolved across different cultures around the world.

Pronunciation guides have been provided as footnotes on the relevant pages for words that may be more difficult to pronounce. These notes are to be used as a guide only and do not reflect regional differences or dialects. Every effort has been made to ensure these guides are simple to use and therefore they do not take into account sounds that are not present within the English language, they have been compiled using words and sounds that children will encounter in their everyday language use.

Why read Myths and Legends?

The ancient stories we call myths and legends are among the oldest creations of the human race. The tale of the hero Gilgamesh, for example, is thought to have been first told in the Middle East over 4000 years ago, long before the earliest mentions of the Greek gods such as Zeus and

Curriculum coverage chart

	Speaking, listening, drama	Reading	Writing
Fables from Africa			
PNS Literacy Framework (Y3)	3.3	**V G** 7.1, 8.1	9.2
National Curriculum	Level 2/3 AF4	Level 2/3 AF1, 2, 3, 7	Level 2/3 AF3
Scotland (P4) (5–14) C for E	Level B/C First Level	Level B/C First Level	Level B/C First Level
N. Ireland (P4/Y4)	Level 2/3	Level 2/3	Level 2/3
Wales (Y3)	Level 2/3 Skills: 3, 4, 5 Range: 3, 4	Level 2/3 Skills: 1, 2, ,3, 4, 5 Range: 1, 2	Level 2/3 Skills: 2, 3, 4, 5, 6 Range: 1, 2, 4
When a Cat Ruled the World			
PNS Literacy Framework (Y3)	4.1	**V G** 7.1, 8.1	9.2
National Curriculum	Level 2/3 AF5	Level 2/3 AF1, 2, 3, 7	Level 2/3 AF3
Scotland (P4) (5–14) C for E	Level B/C First Level	Level B/C First Level	Level B/C First Level
N. Ireland (P4/Y4)	Level 2/3	Level 2/3	Level 2/3
Wales (Y3)	Level 2/3 Skills: 3, 4, 5 Range: 3, 4, 5, 6	Level 2/3 Skills: 1, 2, 3, 4, 5, 7 Range: 1, 2	Level 2/3 Skills: 1, 2, 4, 5, 7 Range: 1, 2, 3, 4

Curriculum coverage chart

Legend:
- **G** = Language comprehension
- **V** = Vocabulary enrichment
- AF = Assessment Focus
- Y = Year   P = Primary

	Speaking, listening, drama	Reading	Writing
Hercules the Hero			
PNS Literacy Framework (Y3)	4.2	**V C** 7.2, 7.5	9.4
National Curriculum	Level 2/3 AF5	Level 2/3 AF1, 2, 3, 5	Level 2/3 AF7
Scotland (P4) (5–14) C for E	Level B/C First Level	Level B/C First Level	Level B/C First Level
N. Ireland (P4/Y4)	Level 2/3	Level 2/3	Level 2/3
Wales (Y3)	Level 2/3 Skills: 3, 4, 5 Range: 3, 4, 5	Level 2/3 Skills: 1, 2, 3, 4, 5, 7 Range: 1, 2	Level 2/3 Skills: 1, 4 Range: 1, 3, 4
King Midas and other Tales			
PNS Literacy Framework (Y4)	1.1, 4.2	**V C** 7.5	9.5
National Curriculum	Level 3/4 AF4	Level 3/4 AF1, 2, 5, 7	Level 3/4 AF7
Scotland (P5) (5–14) C for E	Level B/C First Level/Second Level	Level B/C First Level/Second Level	Level B/C First Level/Second Level
N. Ireland (P5/Y5)	Level 3/4	Level 3/4	Level 3/4
Wales (Y4)	Level 3/4 Skills: 3, 4, 5, 7 Range: 3, 4, 5	Level 3/4 Skills: 1, 2 ,3, 4, 5, 7 Range: 1, 2	Level 3/4 Skills: 1, 2, 3, 7, 8, 9 Range: 1, 2, 3

Curriculum coverage chart

Legend: **C** = Language comprehension; **V** = Vocabulary enrichment; *AF* = Assessment Focus; Y = Year P = Primary

	Speaking, listening, drama	Reading	Writing
How the World Began			
PNS Literacy Framework (Y4)	1.3	**V C** 7.5, 8.2	9.2
National Curriculum	Level 3/4 AF2	Level 3/4 AF1, 2, 5, 7	Level 3/4 AF1
Scotland (P5) (5–14) C for E	Level B/C First Level/Second Level	Level B/C First Level/Second Level	Level B/C First Level/Second Level
N. Ireland (P5/Y5)	Level 3/4	Level 3/4	Level 3/4
Wales (Y4)	Level 3/4 Skills: 3, 4, 5, 7 Range: 3, 4, 5, 6	Level 3/4 Skills: 1, 2, 3, 4, 5, 7, 8 Range: 1, 2	Level 3/4 Skills: 1, 2, 3, 4, 5 Range: 2, 3, 4
Rama's Journey			
PNS Literacy Framework (Y4)	3.1, 4.1	**V C** 7.2, 8.2	9.2
National Curriculum	Level 3/4 AF5	Level 3/4 AF1, 2, 3, 7	Level 3/4 AF1
Scotland (P5) (5–14) C for E	Level B/C First Level/Second Level	Level B/C First Level/Second Level	Level B/C First Level/Second Level
N. Ireland (P5/Y5)	Level 3/4	Level 3/4	Level 3/4
Wales (Y4)	Level 3/4 Skills: 3, 4, 5 Range: 3, 4, 5, 6	Level 3/4 Skills: 1, 2, 3, 4, 5, 7 Range: 1, 2	Level 3/4 Skills: 1 2, 3, 4, 5 Range: 1, 2

Cross-curricular links

TreeTops Myths and Legends Pack 2 Stages 11 and 12	Cross-curricular link
Fables from Africa	**PSHE 2e** Find other fables and discuss how the moral teaches a lesson about how to behave towards others. **Science Sc2 5b** Research the animals from the stories and other animals that live in Africa.
When a Cat Ruled the World	**Geography 2c** Find China, Russia and Britain using an atlas or a globe. **ICT 2a/Drama 4c** Children can create freeze-frame moments from the story. Use a digital camera to photograph the images and use a computer to add captions or thought bubbles.
Hercules the Hero	**Art and Design 1a** Children draw their own superhero. **History 4a** Use the internet to research more information about Ancient Greece. A suitable website is www.bbc.co.uk/schools/ancientgreece.
King Midas and other tales	**Art and Design 1a** Use silver foil to model 3d objects for a class display. **ICT 3a** Display and share the children's stories written on computer with added sounds and images.
How the World Began	**Geography 2c** Find China, North America, Samoa and Australia in an atlas or on a globe. Research countries that can be described as Celtic. Find the names of other islands in the South Pacific.
Rama's Journey	**Geography 2c** Find India in an atlas or on a globe. **Religious Education 1a** Use the internet and texts to find out information about the festivals of Dussehra and Diwali.

Fables from Africa

Author: Timothy Knapman

Synopsis

These five stories from Africa all have a moral. In many of them, animals play tricks on one another.

- *The Tortoise and the Baboon:* Baboon invites Tortoise to dinner, but it is just a trick. Tortoise gets revenge when Baboon has to cross over blackened earth to wash his hands before eating, so never gets his hands clean.

- *The Upside Down Lion:* When Lion is rescued from a trap by a family of warthogs, he plans to eat Baby Warthog. Mrs Warthog tricks Lion back into the trap where he learns his lesson.

- *The Hungry Hyena:* Jackal takes the hungry Hyena to a pen where he can eat his fill of sheep, but it is a trick to divert attention away from the jackal himself.

- *The Bag of Salt:* When Lizard jumps on Tortoise's bag of salt and claims it as his own, the village elders rule that it should be cut in two and shared. Tortoise gets revenge by jumping on Lizard and claiming him as his own and the village elders make the same ruling.

- *Stronger than the Lion:* Hare takes the boastful Lion to a hut to show him something even stronger than Lion and locks him in, so the starving Lion discovers that Hunger is something stronger than he.

Background information

- Animal trickster stories are found in many cultures. These stories have been handed down over a long period and there are many different versions.

- *The Tortoise and the Baboon* is a retelling of a Snapdragons picture book for younger children, with more complex text and less reliance on illustrations.

- *The Upside Down Lion* is often entitled *The Lion and the Mouse*.

- In African myth jackals are usually used to portray characters who outsmart stronger animals by using their wit.

Group or guided reading

Introducing the book

C *(Questioning, Clarifying)* Look at the front cover and read the title. Ask the children what they know about fables. If necessary, explain that fables usually end with a moral or lesson. Invite them to read the letter from the author on page 2.

C *(Predicting)* Ask the children to read the contents page. Ask them if they are familiar with any of the stories and to speculate on what they could be about.

C *(Predicting, Imagining)* Invite the children to describe any fables they have read in the past. Do they think there will be any similarities with these fables?

C *(Clarifying, Questioning)* Invite the children to look briefly through the book, focussing on the illustrations. Discuss how important they think the illustrations are in setting the context of the stories.

Strategy check

V Remind the children to use the sounds of letters to work out new and unfamiliar words. Point to the words 'scampered' on page 4 and 'knobbly' on page 5. Ask volunteers to read the words and to suggest strategies for working them out if children are unsure.

V If the children meet words where the meaning is unclear, remind them to read the whole sentence and work out the meaning from the context.

During reading

C *(Clarifying)* Invite the children to read the two stories that feature a tortoise: *The Tortoise and the Baboon* and *The Bag of Salt*. Explain that you want them to find out what tricks are played on the tortoise and how he gets his own back in each story.

● *(R, AF1)* As the children read independently, listen to them in turn and prompt as necessary. Note the strategies used to decode words.

Independent reading

Objective: Identify and make notes of the main points of sections of text. (7.1).

Clarifying, Summarising

- Ask the children, while they read, to make notes on the tricks that are played in each story and on their similarities and differences.

- When the children have read both stories, ask them to summarise the stories in their own words.

- Invite them to share the notes they made during reading. Ask them to say how Tortoise gets his revenge in both stories. Which one did they prefer and why?

- Invite them to read the remaining three stories.

Assessment: *(R, AF2)* Do the children make sensible, legible notes that they can use to explain their opinion?

Returning and responding to the text

Objective: Share and compare reasons for reading preferences, extending the range of books read. (8.1)

Deducing, Clarifying, Imagining, Summarising

- Turn to page 18. Ask the children what they think Lion is thinking. Ask them to find words or phrases in the text that support their opinions.

- Turn to page 23. Ask the children to find the word 'extraordinary' and describe the strategies used to read it.

- Ask the children to explain why Jackal took Hyena to the pen full of sheep and goats. Ask them if they think Hyena will still be friends with Jackal.

- Invite the children to summarise the story, *Stronger than the Lion*. Do they think Lion will be different after his experience, and if so, how?

- Invite the children to choose the story from the collection they prefer most and to say why.

Assessment: Check that the children:

- *(R, AF2)* can find evidence in the text to support their ideas about each story.
- *(R, AF3)* can deduce reasons why the animals played tricks.
- *(R, AF7)* can identify features that the stories have in common.

Speaking and listening

Objective: Use the language of possibility to investigate and reflect on feelings, behaviour or relationships (3.3).

- Arrange the children into five small groups. Provide each group with a different moral taken from the stories. Ask them to read the moral and to put it into their own words. Ask them to discuss the moral, say whether they agree with it and to describe some possible consequences if the moral were to be ignored.
- Invite each group to summarise their discussion for the other groups.

Assessment: *(S&L, AF4)* Can the children make contributions, share their ideas and respond to others' suggestions?

Writing activites

Objective: Use beginning, middle and end to write narratives in which events are sequenced logically and conflicts resolved (9.2).

- Ask the children to work in pairs and choose one of the stories.

- Ask the children to work together to retell the story orally. Encourage them to sequence the events of their retelling by using a variety of time-based connectives, such as 'when', 'later' and 'suddenly'.

- Invite them to collaborate to write their retellings and then re-read them aloud to each other.

Assessment: *(W, AF3)* Can the children sequence their retellings logically and signal time and place?

Cross-curricular links

PSHE

- Find other fables and discuss how the moral teaches a lesson about how to behave towards others.

Science

- Research the animals from the stories and other animals that live in Africa.

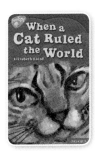

When a Cat Ruled the World

Author: Elizabeth Laird

Synopsis

These three stories are tales from long ago and all feature cats.

- *When a Cat Ruled the World:* In this myth from China, the gods choose a cat to rule the world, but as the cat is too lazy the gods choose people as rulers instead.

- *Samson and the Scaredy Cats:* This folk tale from Russia describes how the animals in the forest talk themselves into believing that Samson the cat is the scariest monster in the world.

- *King of the Cats:* This ghostly folk tale from long-ago Britain describes a strange sight experienced by Peter the gravedigger and its effect on Tom the cat.

Background information

- Cats have played a major part in folklore, myths and legends throughout time.

- Some cultures have revered cats and have stories in which cats are gods.

- Black cats were frequently linked to stories of the supernatural. In some versions of *King of the Cats*, Tom and the cats in the graveyard are black, and some are black with a white spot. Sometimes the coffins are black and in others they are white.

Group or guided reading

Introducing the book

(C) *(Questioning, Clarifying, Predicting)* Look at the front cover and read the title. Invite the children to read the letter from the author on page 2. Read the titles of the stories and ask the children to speculate on what they might be about.

(C) *(Clarifying, Questioning)* Invite the children to look briefly through the book, focusing on the illustrations. Discuss how important they think the illustrations are in setting the context of the stories.

Strategy check

(V) Remind the children to use the sounds of letters to work out new and unfamiliar words. Ask them to suggest other strategies for working out words if they are unsure.

(V) If the children meet words where the meaning is unclear, remind them to read the whole sentence and work out the meaning from the context.

During reading

(C) *(Clarifying)* Invite the children to read the first story, *When a Cat Ruled the World*. Explain that you want them to find out what skill was taken from the cat when the gods chose a different ruler.

(●) *(R, AF1)* As the children read independently, listen to them in turn and prompt as necessary. Note the strategies used to decode words.

Independent reading

Objective: Identify and make notes of the main points of sections of text (7.1).

Summarising

- Ask the children, while they read, to make a note to remind them what the main events were in the beginning, middle and end of the story.
- When the children have read the story, ask them to summarise it in their own words.
- Invite them to share their notes. Ask them what the main events in the beginning, middle and ending were. Have they all made the same or similar notes?
- Invite them to read the remaining two stories.

Assessment: *(R, AF3)* Can the children explain why the cat is described as 'clever'?

Returning and responding to the text

Objective: Share and compare reasons for reading preferences, extending the range of books read. (8.1).

Deducing, Imagining, Summarising

- Invite the children to say which story they enjoyed the most and why. Ask them to describe how the stories differed.
- Turn to page 20. Ask the children why they think the hare told the wolf that a huge beast had leaped on him. Do they think he really believes this happened? Why?
- Turn to page 45. Ask the children if they think the cat can really understand what the gravedigger is saying.

- Invite the children to work with a partner and imagine what the gravedigger and his wife would say to their neighbours the next day.
- Invite the children to summarise the story they enjoyed most to their partner.

Assessment: Check that the children:

- *(R, AF2)* can find evidence in the text to support their ideas about each story.
- *(R, AF7)* can identify how the stories differ.

Speaking and listening

Objective: Present events and characters through dialogue to engage the interest of an audience (4.1).

- Arrange the children into pairs. Ask each pair to choose either *When a Cat Ruled the World* or *King of the Cats*. Explain that you want them to work out a dialogue between either a god and the cat or between the gravedigger and his wife to describe what happens in the story.
- When they have had sufficient time to rehearse, invite each pair to perform their dialogue for the others.

Assessment: *(S&L, AF5)* Can the children perform their dialogues in role?

Writing activites

Objective: Use beginning, middle and end to write narratives in which events are sequenced logically and conflicts resolved (9.2).

- Ask the children to work in pairs and use the notes they made for the beginning, middle and ending of *When a Cat Ruled the World*. Explain they should collaborate to expand their notes, using their own words, and write a paragraph for each section of the story.
- Encourage them to sequence the events of their retelling by using a variety of time-based connectives, such as 'when', 'later' and 'suddenly'.
- Invite the pairs to share their retellings and compare the similarities and differences.

Assessment: *(W, AF3)* Can the children sequence their retellings logically and signal time and place?

Cross-curricular links

Geography
- Find China, Russia and Britain using an atlas or a globe.

ICT/Drama
- Children can create freeze-frame moments from the story. Use a digital camera to photograph the images and use a computer to add captions or thought bubbles.

Hercules the Hero

Author: Michaela Morgan

Synopsis

This legend from Ancient Greece retells the story of how Hercules completed the twelve labours set by Eurystheus, the King of Mycenae.

Background information

- The legend of Hercules is long and complex. Hercules was the illicit son of the god Zeus and Alcmene, a beautiful and wise mortal woman. Zeus's wife, Hera, was furious. When Zeus secretly gave Hercules some of Hera's milk, Hercules became immortal.

- As Hercules grew up he became greater than all other men in size, strength and weaponry skills, but he was dogged by the jealousy of Hera. She could not kill him, since he was immortal, so she vowed to make his life as hard as possible. Under Hera's evil spell he killed his children in a fit of madness. When sanity returned, he went to the Oracle at Delphi to ask how he might atone. The Oracle ordered him to serve Eurystheus, King of Mycenae, for 12 years. It was then that the Oracle gave him the name 'Hercules' (or 'Heracles'), meaning 'glory of Hera'.

Group or guided reading

Introducing the book

C *(Questioning, Clarifying, Predicting)* Look at the front cover and read the title. Ask the children to describe anything they already know about Hercules. Invite them to read the letter from the author on page 2.

C *(Clarifying)* Invite the children to look briefly through the book, focusing on the illustrations. Discuss how important they think the illustrations are in setting the context.

V Turn to page 8. Point out the name Eurystheus and the pronunciation guide (footnote). Help the children pronounce it correctly.

V Turn to page 22. Point out the name Augeas and the pronunciation guide (footnote). Again, help the children say the word.

Strategy check

V Remind the children to use the sounds of letters to work out new and unfamiliar words. Ask the children to suggest other strategies for working out words if they are unsure.

V If the children meet words where the meaning is unclear, remind them to read the whole sentence and work out the meaning from the context.

During reading

C *(Clarifying)* Invite the children to read up to the end of page 25. Explain that when they finish, you want them to describe the task that they think was the worst or most difficult.

● *(R, AF1)* As the children read independently, listen to them in turn and prompt as necessary. Note the strategies used to decode words.

Independent reading

Objective: Infer characters' feelings in fiction and consequences in logical explanations (7.2).

Summarising

- On page 10, encourage the children to read the onomatopoeic words with an expressive tone.

- If any children struggle with 'Hydra' on page 15, encourage them to use the pronunciation guide (footnote).

- When the children have read the story to page 25, ask them to summarise it in their own words.

- Which task do they think is the most difficult and why?

- Before inviting them to read the rest of the story, turn to page 29 and ask the children to point out the word 'Diomedes'. If any of the children have difficulty pronouncing it correctly, ask them to compare the word ending with the word 'Hercules'. Explain that it is a Greek name and the end of the last syllable is pronounced 'eez'. Ask them to find another name in the text with the same spelling/pronunciation pattern (Hades, page 40).

- Turn to page 32. Find the word 'Hippolyte' and help the children pronounce it using the pronunciation guide (footnote).

Assessment: *(R, AF3)* Can the children explain why they chose a particular task as most difficult, using reference to the text?

Returning and responding to the text

Objective: Explore how different texts appeal to readers using varied sentence structures and descriptive language (**7.5**).

Summarising, Questioning, Clarifying, Deducing

- Invite the children to say which part of the story they enjoyed most and why.
- Turn to page 33. Ask the children what 'escaped by a whisker' means.
- Turn to page 38 and ask why Hercules asked for a pillow.
- Turn to page 42. How has the atmosphere or tone of the story changed? Which words in the text illustrate this?
- Ask the children to think about the way the author has written the story. Ask them to describe the overall tone. Is it frightening, exciting, funny, light-hearted? Ask them to find examples of the author's use of language to support their opinions.

Assessment: Check that the children:

- *(R, AF1)* can use appropriate strategies to work out words of Greek origin.
- *(R, AF2)* can find evidence in the text to support their ideas.
- *(R, AF5)* can identify words and phrases the author uses to add humour to the story.

Speaking and listening

Objective: Use some drama strategies to explore stories or issues (**4.2**).

- Ask the children in pairs to think of two questions they would like to ask Hercules about how he completed the tasks. Invite volunteers to hotseat the character of Hercules, and the other children to question him.

Assessment: *(S&L, AF5)* Can the children in the hotseat talk about the tasks from Hercules' point of view using the first person?

Writing activites

Objective: Select and use a range of technical and descriptive vocabulary (9.4).

- Provide the children with large sheets of blank paper. Invite the children to choose one of the monsters from the story. Ask them to draw the monster and find descriptive words and phrases from the story and write these around the picture as labels. Encourage them to add descriptive words of their own.

Assessment: *(W, AF7)* Can the children add imaginative vocabulary of their own to the drawing?

Cross-curricular links

Art and Design

- Children draw their own superhero. Ask them to think about what special skills they will have, what they will wear and what gadgets they will have. Add labels in afterwards.

History

- Use the internet to research more information about Ancient Greece. A suitable website is www.bbc.co.uk/schools/ancientgreece.

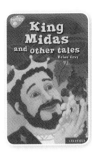

King Midas and other tales

Author: Brian Gray

Synopsis
This book features three stories from around the world that feature prayers, wishes, silver and gold.

- *Silver Tongues:* This is a folk tale from Bolivia. The people of the mountain valley are invaded by cruel, greedy men who force them to work in silver mines under the mountain. When the people pray to the mountain spirits, a stranger comes and helps them rid the valley of the invaders.

- *The Golden Fish:* When Lin Chun is taken away as a slave to build the Great Wall of China, he gives his wife a golden fish with three wishes and warns her never to cry. His wife travels to find him, but when she uses the last wish, she finds that he has died. She then discovers the power of her tears.

- *King Midas:* This is a retelling of the story of how King Midas wished that everything he touched would be turned to gold, with consequences he had not foreseen.

Background information
- Silver from the mountains of Bolivia fuelled the Spanish empire.
- In the building of the Great Wall of China in 200BC, many peasants perished. Some were said to have been entombed within the wall itself. This is a version of

one of the best-known stories about the Great Wall of China, the story of a girl called Meng Jiang Nü.

- Midas was a king whose foolish acts annoyed the gods. Not only did his wish for gold cause him distress, but he also fell into an argument with Apollo about a singing contest and had his ears turned into those of a mule.

- In this retelling Silenus is depicted as a satyr, whereas in some versions he is assisted by them.

Group or guided reading

Introducing the book

C *(Questioning, Clarifying)* Look at the front cover and read the title. Ask the children if they know anything about King Midas.

C *(Questioning, Predicting, Imagining)* Read the contents list and ask the children to speculate on what the stories might be about. Invite them to read the letter from the author on page 2.

C *(Clarifying)* Invite the children to look briefly through the book, focusing on the illustrations. Discuss how important they think the illustrations are in setting the contexts.

Strategy check

V Remind the children to use the sounds of letters to work out new and unfamiliar words. Find the names of the mountains on page 4. Help the children to say the words using the pronunciation guide (footnotes).

V Point to the words 'armour' and 'scoured' on page 5. Ask volunteers to read the words and suggest strategies for working them out if the children are unsure.

V If the children meet words where the meaning is unclear, remind them to read the whole sentence and work out the meaning from the context.

During reading

C *(Clarifying)* Invite the children to read the first story, *Silver Tongues*. Explain that you want them to note any references to silver in the text.

● *(R, AF1)* As the children read independently, listen to them in turn and prompt as necessary. Note the strategies used to decode words.

Independent reading

Objective: Explain how writers use figurative and expressive language to create images and atmosphere (7.5).

Clarifying

● Point out the simile on page 3 'like silver ribbons'. While the children read, ask them to identify other examples of figurative language.

● When the children have read the story, invite them to share the notes they made during reading. Discuss how the author uses silver both literally and figuratively and its effect on the atmosphere.

● Invite the children to read the remaining two stories independently.

Assessment: *(R, AF5)* Can the children identify similes in the text?

Returning and responding to the text

Objective: Explain how writers use figurative and expressive language to create images and atmosphere (7.5).

Clarifying, Deducing, Imagining

- Focus on the story, *The Golden Fish*. Read *The First Emperor*, TreeTops *Graphic Novels*, stage 13, which gives more background information about the building of the Great Wall of China.

- Ask the children to explain why Lin Han asked the emperor to grant the three conditions before she would marry him.

- Ask the children to explain the significance of the gold and the silver fish.

- Turn to page 43. Invite the children to explain why Midas decided to list things that should not turn to gold.

- Turn to page 48. Why did everyone hold their breath when Midas patted the courtier?

- Invite the children to choose one story from the collection that they prefer and to give reasons for their choice.

Assessment: Check that the children:

- *(R, AF2)* can find evidence in the text to support their ideas about each story.

- *(R, AF5)* can explain how the author's use of language affects the atmosphere of the stories.

- *(R, AF7)* can identify features that the stories have in common.

Speaking and listening

Objective: Offer reasons and evidence for their views, considering alternative opinions (1.1). Develop scripts based on improvisation (4.2).

- Discuss which story would be the best to turn into a play and ask the children to give reasons for their opinions. Using the story that the majority chose (probably *King Midas*), arrange the children into groups and ask them to allocate roles and improvise the story.
- Invite the groups to perform their improvisations and compare their similarities and differences.

Assessment: *(S&L, AF4)* Can the children work together to allocate roles and plan their improvisations?

Writing activites

Objective: Choose and combine words, images and other features for particular effects (9.5).

- Ask the children to work in pairs and choose one of the stories. Remind them of the authors' use of figurative language.
- Ask them to collaborate to rewrite the story on a computer, using their own words and including similes and metaphors. Encourage them to experiment by adding images and sounds to create atmosphere.

Assessment: *(W, AF7)* Can the children include similes and metaphors?

Cross-curricular links

Art and Design

- Use silver foil to model 3-dimensional objects for a classroom display.

ICT

- Display and share the children's stories written on a computer with added sounds and images.

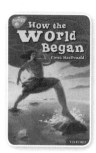

How the World Began

Author: Fiona MacDonald

Synopsis

This book features five creation myths from around the world.

- *Pan Gu and the Egg:* The world is formed when a giant named Pan Gu breaks out of an egg. The eggshell becomes the sky and earth, while Pan Gu's body becomes the many features of the earth and sky.

- *Moon and Morning Star:* At first the world was in darkness. Then, when the first ever people, called Man-Who-Brings-Light and Shining Woman, first wake, their dreams have created everything they need to help the world come to life.

- *Oran Mor:* This Celtic myth describes 'The Song of Life' created by the goddess when she took pity on the dead world that had no water.

- *Tagaloa's Rock:* This myth tells how Tagaloa first created the sky and then the sea. He grew tired, so created an island to rest on. He then created all the islands of the South Pacific.

- *Something Special:* This Aboriginal myth describes how two god spirits, called the Brothers, scraped the mud from two 'Somethings' to discover the first humans.

Background information

- *Pan Gu and the Egg:* First written down by Chinese monks in the third century BC, but probably about a thousand years older. Pan Gu's division of the egg into earth and sky parallels the Chinese philosophical concept of Yin and Yang. (Yin = dark, passive, damp, female; Yang = light, active, dry, male.) As well as creating the world, Pan Gu's action also creates order from chaos.

- *Moon and Morning Star:* This is a Wichita Native American myth, whose traditional homeland is in Oklahoma and Southern Texas, in North America. It tells of a world in which there is a great Creator Spirit and also supernatural beings, such as Moon and Morning Star, who act as messengers, teachers and guardians. It includes the idea of knowledge and skill as gifts to be shared, and for which people should be thankful. Traditionally, maize (corn on the cob) was the staple food of Native American farming peoples living in temperate/warm climates. In this myth, women share responsibility, and have important – but different – tasks. Historically, many Native American women played an active part in farming.

- *Oran Mor:* This creation myth is closely aligned with the ancient Celtic or Druidic religions. It means 'The Song of Life', sometimes called 'The Great Melody'.

- *Tagaloa's Rock:* A myth from Samoa, a group of islands in the Pacific Ocean. It explains how Samoa and many other Pacific islands came to be created and populated. Many different versions of the myth exist. In some, Tagaloa creates the sea and sky as well as dry land; in others, he creates just the Polynesian islands. But the story of how he created people from worms spawned by leaves is widespread.

- *Something Special:* In this Aboriginal myth, the Brothers (guardian gods/spirits) uncover and foster human life (they do not create it). Their full name is the Numbakulla brothers. The myth describes the unity of people and nature. The 'Somethings' (first humans) become the ancestors of the Arrernte people of Central Australia. This myth links to the wider Aboriginal concept of the Dreamtime. This is an ecstatic/magical experience, often called an 'eternal present', in which all of creation is continually celebrated and renewed.

Group or guided reading

Introducing the book

C *(Questioning, Clarifying, Predicting)* Look at the front cover and read the title. Read the contents list and ask the children to speculate on what the stories might be about. Do they think the stories will all describe the same thing? If necessary, explain that these are creation myths. Invite them to read the letter from the author on page 2.

C *(Clarifying)* Invite the children to look briefly through the book, focusing on the illustrations. Discuss how important they think the illustrations are in setting the contexts.

Strategy check

V Remind the children to use the sounds of letters to work out new and unfamiliar words. Point to the words 'surrounded' on page 4 and 'dreadfully' on page 5. Ask volunteers to read the words and suggest strategies for working them out if the children are unsure.

V If the children meet words where the meaning is unclear, remind them to read the whole sentence and work out the meaning from the context.

During reading

C *(Clarifying)* Invite the children to read *Pan Gu and the Egg* and *Tagaloa's Rock* first. Explain that you want them to identify similarities and differences in the two stories.

- *(R, AF1)* As the children read independently, listen to them in turn and prompt as necessary. Note the strategies used to decode words.

Independent reading

Objective: Interrogate texts to deepen and clarify understanding and response (8.2).

Questioning, Clarifying, Deducing

- Provide the children with the following questions to help them find the common elements and the differences:
What sort of being is the creator in these stories?
What is created first?
Why did Pan Gu need to rest?
Why did Tagaloa need to rest?
How did Pan Gu create the features of the earth?
How did Tagaloa create the features of the earth?
What is created in each story?

- When the children have read the stories, invite them to share their opinions about the similarities and differences, showing evidence in the text.

- Invite the children to read the remaining stories independently.

Assessment: *(R, AF2)* Can the children scan the text to find answers to the questions?

Returning and responding to the text

Objective: Explain how writers use figurative and expressive language to create images and atmosphere (7.5).

Clarifying, Deducing, Imagining

- Focus on the story, *Moon and Morning Star.*

- Look at page 15. Ask the children to explain how the author contrasts what the Great Spirit can see and what the world was like in the dark.

- On pages 23–24, how does the author's description make the children feel? Why does the author end the page with an ellipsis?

- Focus on *Oran Mor*. Ask the children to say what the difference is in the sentences on page 27 and those on page 28. Why do they think the author used short and incomplete sentences, then long sentences when the goddess starts the rain?

- Focus on *Something Special* and turn to page 53. Ask the children to describe the effect of the words 'squelchy', 'quivering' and 'trembling'. How do these words make them feel?

- Invite the children to choose the story from the collection they prefer and to give reasons for their choice.

Assessment: Check that the children:

- *(R, AF2)* can find evidence in the text to support their ideas about each story.

- *(R, AF5)* can explain how the author's use of language affects the atmosphere of the stories.

- *(R, AF7)* can identify common features of the stories.

Speaking and listening

Objective: Tell stories effectively and convey detailed information coherently for listeners (1.3).

- Ask the children to work with a partner. Invite them each to choose a different story and, using the illustrations as a prompt, retell the story. Encourage them to add detail and expressive language. Ask them to evaluate each other's use of story language and sequencing of events

Assessment: *(S&L, AF2)* Can the children listen carefully to each other's retellings and comment effectively?

Writing activites

Objective: Use settings and characterisation to engage readers' interest **(9.2)**.

- Discuss an imaginary world without water, plants, animals or people with the children. Draw up a list of their ideas. Ask them to imagine a being that can bring the world to life. Draw up a list of their different ideas about how the being would act.

- Invite the children to write a paragraph describing the setting (the world before life) and another paragraph sketching the character of their being.

Assessment: *(W, AF1)* Can the children use imaginative and expressive descriptions of their own or do they borrow their descriptions from the text?

Cross-curricular links

Geography

- Find China, North America, Samoa and Australia in an atlas or on a globe.

- Research countries that can be described as Celtic.

- Find the names of other islands in the South Pacific.

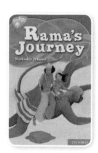

Rama's Journey

Author: Narinder Dhami

Synopsis

When King Das decides to give up the throne in favour of his favourite son Rama, Queen Kaik forces him to send Rama away. Rama, his wife Sita, and brother, Laxman, go and live in the forest where a ten-headed demon called Ravana kidnaps Sita. Rama and Laxman meet a magical monkey who helps them to defeat Ravana and his army, and to rescue Sita.

Background information

- This story retells the Ramayana, which means 'Rama's Journey' or 'Rama's Way'.

- The story of the Ramayana was written, in Sanskrit, by the poet Valmiki. It was probably passed on orally before being written down.

- Some of the names have been simplified in this retelling. In the original story Laxman was called Lakshmana, King Das was King Dasharatha and Queen Kaik was Queen Kaikeyi.

- The Ramayana works on many different levels. It is a thrilling story for children, but its main purpose is to demonstrate the power of good over evil. It is an integral part of the Hindu religion.

- Two of India's annual festivals have their origins in the story of the Ramayana: Dussehra celebrates the slaying of Ravana; Diwali celebrates Rama's return to his kingdom from exile.

Group or guided reading

Introducing the book

(C) *(Questioning, Clarifying, Predicting)* Look at the front cover and read the title. Ask the children if they know anything about the story of Rama. If they are not familiar with it, explain its origin using the background information. Ask them to read the letter from the author and predict what might happen in the story.

(C) *(Clarifying)* Invite the children to look briefly through the book, focusing on the illustrations. Discuss how important they think the illustrations are in setting the context.

Strategy check

(V) Remind the children to use the sounds of letters to work out new and unfamiliar words, including the characters' names. Ask volunteers to suggest strategies for working out new words if the children are unsure.

(V) If the children meet words where the meaning is unclear, remind them to read the whole sentence and work out the meaning from the context.

During reading

(C) *(Clarifying)* Invite the children to read up to the end of Chapter 4. Explain that when they have finished you want them to describe how Ravana managed to kidnap Sita.

(●) *(R, AF1)* As the children read independently, listen to them in turn and prompt as necessary. Note the strategies used to decode words.

Independent reading

Objective: Deduce characters' reasons for behaviour from their actions (7.2).

Questioning, Clarifying, Deducing, Imagining

- On page 9, ask the children why there was nothing the King could do about the Queen's demands.

- On page 20, ask the children why Rama thought there was a trap.

- At the end of Chapter 4, ask the children to suggest what Rama and Laxman might be thinking when the monkey begins to grow. What might happen next?

- Invite the children to continue reading to the end of the story.

Assessment: *(R, AF3)* Can the children refer to other parts of the text to help them understand why the King could not refuse the Queen's demand?

Returning and responding to the text

Objective: Interrogate texts to deepen and clarify understanding and response (8.2).

Clarifying, Questioning, Summarising, Deducing

- Ask the children to return to Chapter 5. Ask them to describe what happened when Rama and Laxman climbed onto Hanuman's shoulders. How was Sita kept in the palace?

- Turn to pages 40–41. Ask the children why Hanuman let the demons catch him and why he pretended to be frightened.

- Turn to page 47. How did the characters reach the island? Invite the children to suggest why Hanuman didn't fly them to the island.

- Ask the children to summarise the last chapter in their own words. Encourage them to link the events without using the phrase 'and then'.

- Invite the children to describe the setting of the story, and to comment on how the story might be different if set in Britain today.

Assessment: Check that the children:

- *(R, AF1)* can make use of a range of strategies to read for meaning.

- *(R, AF2)* can find evidence in the text to support their ideas about the story.

- *(R, AF7)* can identify features of the story that would change if placed in a different setting.

Speaking and listening

Objective: Create roles showing how behaviour can be interpreted from different viewpoints (4.1). Take different roles in groups (3.1).

- Invite volunteers to take turns and sit in the hot seat in the role of Ravana. Ask 'Ravana' to justify his actions in the story. Encourage the others to ask questions about the reasons for his actions.

- Working in groups, invite the children to put Ravana on trial for kidnapping Sita. Ask them to allocate roles including witnesses and a judge.

Assessment: *(S&L, AF5)* Can the children explore the story from Ravana's point of view?

Writing activites

Objective: Use settings and characterisation to engage readers' interest (9.2).

- Invite the children to reread pages 16–17. Discuss the atmosphere of the forest setting. Why did the author end the description with the last paragraph?

- Ask the children to write a description using their own words to show a calm and beautiful forest setting. Explain that the description must end with an element of threat that will make readers want to turn the page.

Assessment: *(W, AF1)* Can the children use imaginative language to build an atmosphere?

Cross-curricular links

Geography

- Find India in an atlas or on a globe.

Religious Education

- Use the internet and texts to find out about the festivals of Dussehra and Diwali.